MW01087361

Typesetting by Janice Lee
Cover Design by Janice Lee
Copyediting by Gabriela Torres Olivares (Spanish)
and Esa Grigsby (English)
ISBN 978-1-948700-17-7

THE ACCOMPLICES:
A #RECURRENT Book

theaccomplices.org

THE ACCOMPLICES

LOSING MIAMI

by Gabriel Ojeda-Sagué

Being that this book is as much about leaving Miami as it is about losing it,
this book is for Y'hoshua, Sarah, Brandon, Rebecca, Patrick, the Suarezes, Kyle, Amanda and the many friends that guided me.

One way to erase an island is to invent
a second island absolved of all the sounds
the first one ever made.
–Patrick Rosal, "Instance of an Island"

A Note on Language

If this book had stage directions, they would read:

6:30 p.m. in Pinecrest Bakery. Ordering pastries in a whisper.

If the reference to Pinecrest Bakery is lost on you, no problem. It will be lost on everybody soon enough! I'm sorry, I don't mean to be flippant, but I also do.

This book is written in the language ecosystem I grew up in: school in English, home in Spanish, the rest of the world in Spanglish. This life was folded, doubled, bent over, over-dubbed.

This book is written in both English and Spanish. There is no English version of this book and no Spanish version of this book.

To those who do not speak Spanish: don't be scared or put off. If you are scared, it's okay. If you are not scared, perhaps you should be. This book is written with fake blood and trick knives.

The feeling of tourism as you move through this book is one I'd like you to remember. This book will not make you a Cubano, nor will it take you to the beach. It will, however, take you to the dream of a beach. Remember that feeling.

(I never really loved Cubanos anyways. Real 305ers eat medianoches.)

I have prepared an Appendix that correctly translates the Spanish of this book, for all who may need that or who may simply be curious of how I'd translate this book. Definition will never be alien to you. But, do not assume that this appendix is free of booby traps. I'm a lover of a bear trap hidden in claptrap.

To any native bilinguals, welcome. I wrote this book in the living room of your childhood home.

Home is never here very long.

Para los que sólo hablan español, llámenme. Les daré todos mis secretos, pero no puedo aquí.

I don't mean to say that the language in this book here is a *realistic* portrayal of the language ecosystem of Miami. First of all, it lacks Haitian Creole, which is essential to Miami's world of sounds. Instead, I mean to say that the language of this book is a hallucination of Miami's language as I experienced it growing up.

All this being said, I hope all readers come to understand that the loss I worry over here is also one of the ear.

LOSING MIAMI

I.

start with sinking:

I was raised in a city
that could be swallowed
by the sea within
the next century

start there

I rest in the sake
of returning,
like drinking from the well

    my spirit talks
    slobber-mouthed
    to you

        to see a ficus
        as the memory of an ocean

there is no shape to the frenetic
odd nerves, the dogs on the other side
of the fence, the thin film on the water,
a single green bump in the middle,
waiting with one eye open:
      need for food

                  I am hopeful about bakeries
                  where periods hang like pearls
                  one word aiming at another

solo lo plástico
sobrevive
     como siempre

así forma un merengue
de botellas sobre el agua

those shopping malls I used
to walk around in, buying nothing,
keep changing stores
a bird is full of egg whites
and sings
little remnants of the yard

picking up pumpkin seeds off the side
of the road
where a woman was betrayed
throwing shells

a la puerta
le meto los cuernos

el océano abrevia
los rastros

little twisting keratin

I mistake one verb for another
unfortunate practice

butter f l
y
m
y
b
a
c
k

an eel sleeping in another eel
I want to think better

                    not a way to walk
      wading through limestone

what the alligator wants
what residency is in its jaw

el avión
el avión
avispaaaaaaa

         I've got the name
         of an angel and windows
         with shutters, I've got a secret
         combination that I keep under my tile floor
         will you put your nose into
         my vents they keep smelling
         like humidity, I really could
         use your help

an eel sleeeeeeeeeeeping

I am asked if I would go to Cuba now that policies have changed. When I ask my abuela the same question, exchanging "irías" for "volverías," she says que "no tengo nada que hacer en Cuba." Somehow, I feel the same, even if I could never say "volvería" because I have never been to Cuba. Returning would not be the form, in my case. But to grow up in Miami, as the child of exiles, is to always be "returning" to Cuba. Everything has a fragrant—not aftertaste, but third taste—of Cuba. Angel Dominguez writes "What is the function of writing? To return (home)" but his gambit is that the flight (home) is the writing, the verb "to return" is the writing, not the home itself or returning to it. What is the function of writing: "to return." The answer is no, I would not go to Cuba, because the Cuba I come from only can be returned to in the murmurs of the exile.

I wonder what it would be like to be exiles from Miami, to have the city be an effect only of memory and simulation as Havana is for the Cuban exile generation, to have any description of the city be a dangling modifier, to have to put my antennae at the bottom of the ocean.

just as much as me and more

Francisco, bring me a tissue
I want to clean up the hairs on the floor
of the bathroom

I want my friend to see me as someone
he could love, I mean really love

I want to get squeezed till I turn out
dented like a pipe

if a lizard gets in the door
get him with a napkin
let him live
get him with a napkin

river monsters
  trudge
   behind
     pink
           life

ghostly guilt harmonics

here is my selfish life
          it is in your hands

as light as the Keys
and more so

1) Imagine the loss of something small.

2) Imagine the loss of something about your size.

3) Imagine the loss of something very large.

Do you imagine these differently? Is one more
possible than another? What bodily responses
do you have? Have you felt such things before?
What are your first, most immediate memories
of these losses? Once my neighbor lost a watch,
once my neighbor lost his father, once my neighbor
lost his house when a ficus fell on it.

THE THOUSANDS

I Do Not

I do not wake up alone here. There is a vital sign, the noon notes at the church, sediment to open the day. It won't be cold. A solution of red water and eroded shell. Lacking the screen to see, I place my shoulder against the beach. Praise the swollen bird and the devil's belly. Hungry for the scene, or in time for it. A cashbox. Does the apartment building above me wrinkle the ground to keep me company? It's tall for the sake of the beach. I'm letting myself crisp. I am not far from a bronze boy in a speedo who doesn't smile at me. We're both hoping a silver rubber band would cut through the water. Someone woke up at the same time as me and is still awake. My ears heat up when I'm embarrassed; I'm embarrassed now. Isn't it going to stop? Mustn't it not get worse? Certain of little sand cities, a kid is welcoming waves, saying (once under his breath, once aloud) that they are strong enough. Plane's banner ad, GIRLS GET IN FREE, velour in its reflection over the water. Certainly I stumble, am not married, am obsessed with haircuts. Shirtless disco. Have taken time to appear to be a Google image lawn mole. Painting of "surface" lies low. Beachgoers are a plain resource, iron-willed, cream-covered, ore veins. This beach's Newton is an umbrella.

It ignores the problem of bottles. There are several levels to self-doubt, but none of them are special. Sandcastle kid sets his thumb in a paper project, craft moons, that he is lining up in a thick row. He throws one up and hopes it sticks. I hate to say it, but I have trouble balancing how much I want to leave with how much I don't want to leave. Titles to waltzing edge. This thin line for the crab; this, that, and mine. And so, if you ask me if I feel calm, I do not. Cotton displays his discomfort. I want every inch of this to live. Sleeptalking, I leave the beach, find I've parked a hundred times in a circle. Send help to me and the museum. Send $50, bottles of soap, wreaths, plantains, advertisements, extra headspace, and validated tickets to my family. Ignore birds. Think more on it and then get back to me. Lie under my tongue. I look back at the water and turn into an accidental jetty. Swollen overnights. Locked a red light in the face of holy Hummer throwing ice on my windshield. Need constantly to U-turn. Have noticed a drain where there wasn't one before; have noticed a second "No Left Turn." This way leads over and around the backside of US-1 and lets me out in a blender. Green apathy, watered by people we euphemistically call "the city." I am told by a gorgeous straight man that it is all about taxes. That we can make money differently. That gentrifiers are buying higher altitude property and pushing the poor to lower altitude neighborhoods where houses will be lost first. He tells me there are many pipelines towards central and that I deserve to bundle them as hair in my fist. He says, petting his dog, this one and that one are friends, and that we all have septic tanks, which is true. They are softer than I think. He says here's to a pour. In lightning, I keep my glove compartment. He's safe from mangrove hunting. Flintstones on lime. Feeling dim. Family portrait of my brother gargling through his fingers. Irregular neutral lets the car roll back even on flat ground. Brings me back over the causeway, up a drawbridge, and falling into the bay. I'm the bath salts cannibal when I'm in my car. I've said it before. And so, if you ask me if I usually act this way, I do not. The cold ring on my neck is rising, and not as slow as once we thought. I have both hands on my shoulders, not on the wheel, and I am determined to hyphenate. Spread RPM across the university and into my home. A goldfish with me in the living room loses memory from one side to another. Blue buffoon. Pixelated opera in my DVR, asking in an aria why love is papery. Desperation formed out of the midday. Light and water. I live on Ancona Ave, not in a snow globe. And I believe certainly that things move fast. The cold ring rises over street signs, which are quite near the floor. It's moving up and down my forearms quickly, cooling me down and exciting me. I'll make this an allergic reaction. Toys on the shelf. Fruit hanging in a Jell-O mold. Squeeze out eye drops onto this book and pray for me. I never thought that my ruling planet would not be a planet. That water would come through a glove of plastic into my window. That people would spread their hands wide and narrow into the globe's raw portion and bring out a wound.

Never thought that and never thought I'd be at home for it. That minor gasp. Thinking of you constantly. I need the chance to explain myself, to say that I'm anxious and in love in my room. Slivers of grease spilled on the carpet. Streams in the desert. Hardly a bushel of ideas pronounced throughout the day. Making Memorial Day at home a dizzy family barbeque. Knuckles on Vaseline. Who we called "Key rats." Who we didn't. "Damp, which is the most insidious of all enemies…damp steals in while we sleep." This is all PR. They are putting up signs that say "the problem is being solved" and "please still visit" and asking you for a check. They are saying they are working. They are saying that they are reading the exclamation of pipelines. None of this is true. Permacrumble. I'm opening a hole in PR. Miami would like you to visit. Would like too to build new buildings. To propose overcrowding. This traffic here is the product of geese fighting. This traffic here is the product of a new road. This traffic here is the product of rain. This traffic here is the product of several flat tires. None of it has to do with the thousands of people on this very highway. None of it is my fault. In my CRV, I'm the king of clogged spitball straw. Rest your head on my shoulder as we wait it out. We wait out that growing white noise of leaks in drains below. White noise of septic tanks bursting. Of limestone cut into. Of shuffling beachgoers. Of construction. Of a pots and pans riot. Of the humble sound of a glass reed blown into for a clarinet. We wait it out and drive. And so, if you ask me if I feel at home, I do not. And this is really the worst time of the year, when it rains every day for five minutes. Telemarketer's paradise. Kind of tranquil. I'm foamy and repentant. This packet and package. Turning oil over. As if to be well read was to move inland. That's a joke. Here's another: mail to Cuba. Knowing the same thing every day is the rash along both arms. Remembering the same thing every day. The rash along both arms. "Spelling the death of." This, that, and that one "spell the death of." I am writing this and the president has just said he will pull out of the Paris Agreement. What a job. I hate to admit it, but I'm not trying to make a change, I'm trying to grieve. Is this house occupied or stoned? In pictures, spelled out, a message between two imagined people. Will the Senator take the floor? View of the water from the advertising plane, the stoop to absent wind-chill. Driving back again to the beach, a diorama of pinched skin in the passenger seat. Island means dying today, coast tomorrow. Somewhat overdrawn. For the sake of going on, I build property. I make money as I build and so I build more. I'm both the ghosts that live in the Biltmore and the shell of veterans too. The gorgeous straight man says we need to make money differently, that I should be subsidized for connecting to the sewage system, that all productive change is a billboard, and that Rick Scott is a Nazi. I pet his dog as we wait out the white noise. He admits that I'm the only one between us that can say I've had many enemies in a small, religious space. Glorious yearbook. Head of the lizard. What I feel at thinking of holding nothing.

When I won't be. My friend says she won't ever have children because of what is happening in the world. On the other hand, I can do nothing but rear. Maps of a mirror. After we're done with this, give me a long book to skim. Certain of where to go. Betting on temporary, from the balcony of a rich girl. Hoping it will storm to see a yarn ball held low above dark blue. Tormenting. Hoping I'll find myself a rut and explode. Push peanuts out of my hand. Cause friends to swell. Don't tell me that it's literally all my actions causing this, even if it is. I can't figure that one. Instead, be honest and tell me it is ones with larger influence. Ribcages of corporations. Day to day in a government. Hands with lacking. This nasty segment. Piece of a pill. Cutting into the cake. Graphics of a motorboat. Cutting green into a manatee back. This ear of mine, full of sand, is not telling time. I do not wake up alone here, alone in thinking I am losing everything. And so, if you ask me if I think things will improve, I do not. Fingers on the forceps of a fence. Being vodka for my St. Bernard. These hollow blinking holes in my foot, stinging from salt coming in, going out. I'm the red wolf turned gray at 1AM, spinning hectically towards my tail. At night, losing one or more of my senses comes as no surprise.

Relieve Himself

If a man is seen fighting with another one over parking
and another man curses in Spanish over everyone yelling
and another man is hiding in the corner not involved
and another man is covering his kid's ears
and another man punches another man, repeatedly
and another man is eating a medianoche, watching
and another man is drunk, watching
and another man is waiting to pass
and another man is allowing this to happen, as the rest
and another man is a security guard
and another man is another security guard
and another man is asked if he needs help
and another man who is a security guard is cruel
and another man who is a security guard has a short temper
and another man who is a security guard beats a man
and another man is arrested for violence
and another man is put in the back of a car
and another man is cursing "¡'ño!" or "hijo'e puta"

and another man is not invested
and another man is taking his kid for ice cream
and another man is drunk, watching
and another man is not sure where he is going in that car
and another man is sure where he is going in that car
and another man is feeling betrayed
and another man is feeling victorious
and another man is feeling agonized
and another man is feeling anxious
and another man is inhumane
and another man is taking sharp turns
and another man is bleeding from his head
and another man is sitting on a curb with a security guard
and another man is offering another man first aid
and another man is saying "pendejo"
and another man is saying "maricón"
and another man is saying "cabrón"
then the parking lot is relieved
because it has done its job

Fire Ants

what a weak theory I have built for myself
the daily hurricane in the refrigerator
not yet condensed
the ziploc of fire ants
my tendency to trill
warmth against the door
I built such a life out of life, its doctored complications
I made this
these shapes of thin cheeks
I made the tropics into a thin circular theorem
but with a hand in their pincers
I'm starting to connect allergens
to form a pyramid

The Thousands

reflected or drowning, thousands are moving along a barbed line

***

life is thicker here in the cock state

fireworks in the dreams of thousands

I have not made this up

vertebrae tercet

after electricity, there is food, golden-spiced

slow moving hands

they have told me and I have seen

that thousands don't leave

that everywhere is different and unimaginable

that everywhere is somewhere else unimaginable

thousands pray to stay, to live here again

this cannot go

flat

absent

state

I say doldrums as if it were not my liver's curse

pushing sky into sky

to not see sky is to rotate a plane

so I rotate a plane

the war occurred here in the homes of thousands

it was fought in jowls

thousands are playing dominoes

bloom touching

absolute value

negative rehearsal

search a symphony for the absence of everything

to find spittle on the floors

it makes small triangles, brilliantly coral

that I pinch into my abdomen

and warm between my ribs

bloom touching

absolute organ

I'd rather dry up the entire world

than see one drop in the mouth of thousands

Down

lord god a woman flew
down on a cloud to put me back in the box
in the alleyway in the shit neighborhood
lord god there were
people there and cats
lord god that is where I gained weight
lord god that is where the sea starts
lord god a woman flew
down on a cloud
I love all the people I'm
around all the time
give me the gulf in a paper bag

The Organization of Cobras

pulse drive is available only for wet feet, dry feet
the glass bulbs shifting across 90 miles
of a sweet pale sheet of flood covered in confetti
will be accepted by an organization of cobras
all others will not
please come simply as you are

Beaches

along the beach another yellower beach on top
the mirror image
tourist soda fizz
I want what I want
sourness of algae
be my friend
this place is a gorgeous index
I'll ask again
along the beach another yellower oxidized beach on top
crawling over it
diamonds along the sand
on the second beach no trace of a dog
or those little white birds that go in and out
people only thousands of them
I didn't dream them up
flat absent state
distinct smell of the shape it takes under direct light
above ground above image

I have placed thousands of bottles into the strait as
morse code for you my island neighbor
to say “everywhere bilingual must go”
a girl is wishing she was a fish
she will get her wish
a series of small triangles
chrome-colored and alien
lift out of the ocean to take crumbs
from a beachgoer’s tote bag

LOSING MIAMI

II.

see with wonder, my only healer
no love for my only healer
my only hairs pile onto my back
my only finger's way to pointing

I want every baby on
earth to be born in Miami,
and then I want it to leave at
18 and want Miami back

nothing grows here
but hopes for growing

You gotta want something back.
If you wanna have my heart,
you gotta want something back.

We are sitting in a burger place in Coconut Grove, talking about coffee and how I don't like to drink it, when you pull out a red jar. You tell me about it in detail. I imagine if I broke it and how you would feel about that. I laugh at the part when you mention how much it cost you and the waitress mentions how she saw a similar one for a lower price, but not at The Container Store. You ask me what is so funny, outside of my dream, and I say that the jar reminded me of a friend who was funny. You open the jar and say that it is nothing like my friend and it isn't very funny. I see what you mean now and I'm sorry for the way I acted earlier.

In Key Largo, where you mentioned we shouldn't go, and were right, there was a big man in a blue suit, which looked too warm for Key Largo weather. You said you didn't like the way I was sitting. I open up the trunk of my car and stuff you in it. You are very nostalgic about that moment, still.

As I'm driving down the Palmetto, I see a roach on the passenger's seat. I just freak out and start swerving. I kill a family of four with my CRV because I am very afraid of roaches.

In Miami, I have a yellow house. Right now, I am staying in a purple house. You can't tell either of these colors at night, which disappoints me. I open a pack of Mentos Gum as if to say "I only came here on a whim." There is a raccoon in the swale and it's a Monday, so he won't last very long.

I find hair in a plastic bag of food I brought from your friend's house. Not a strand, but a thick lock of hair, of your friend's mother's hair. I later find out that it was the new maid who cut it off in the middle of the night and was saving it for a ritual. When I look down your friend's street, there is a single man waving. You wish you knew as much as she does about sage.

There are several boxes we have to move out of your apartment that have been there very long. When we lift one, together, there are silverfish moving under it. You say "silverfish are a way of showing you something is filthy." I don't think the box has anything in it, but it still needs to be moved for being a box. The neighbor knocks on the walls again because I am making her baby cry.

During the night, I often pull out your hairs and blame it on little ghosts.

I imagine what you would think if I got HIV from a mutual friend. I get stumped because I remember that at this stage in our lives we have no other gay friends. I still think you'd be rather disappointed, but maybe not in me.

As you warned me, I am becoming allergic to dogs. The other day, I went to a good friend's house and played with his dog. I didn't tell you I was going, but I played with his dog. Soon enough, when the dog humped my leg, I swelled up and became very pale. My pinkies fell off and my good friend told me that I was exaggerating. I tried to call someone and tell them that my pinkies had fallen off and that I was very big and very white because of my good friend's dog, but everyone didn't answer and you had just rewired all my phone calls to you to taxi companies instead, as you often did. It took me two weeks of Vick's Vapo Rub to get the color back into my cheeks.

In poetry, I have found very many communists. In Miami, my grandfather tells me again about seeing Che shooting people just outside his street. This time he gets the dates exactly right.

In South Beach, I buy myself a new face.

Your mother cooks me eggs and asks me what Gucci purse she should get rid of and which she should keep. But you and I know that there isn't a real version of "get rid of." The view from your apartment, or your old apartment, is stunning. I can make out even the signs by Publix, where it says, "No Left Turn."

Before we go to sleep, your divider door slides open and there's a very old man with a very bad burn there. He says he misses the "old you," but I feel confused about what that means. I get so mad at you for keeping him from me that I start to pee on the carpet when you aren't looking. You cover it with a lemon scent that you say reminds you of your last apartment. Or was it the one before the last one? Or the other one?

This really is where US-1 ends. Did you think I was kidding?

If it is nighttime, I have planned leaving my room and getting to the kitchen for a snack several times so far. I know just how to turn on each light so that there is never a dark room ahead of me. I close my windows quickly, in case someone is watching. I close my door so that I can't see into the hallway. I make sure my phone is facing down so that I don't confuse the light for anything else. I have to lie on my back to make sure nothing is creeping up on either side of me.

I live in Coral Gables, where you can't see the street signs. But I know exactly where to turn and I will tell you when you are getting close.

ask again for
return instructions,
be put on hold,
wait one hundred years,
resume your call
at the start of a new shoreline
pull the phone wire through the flotsam:
once I got my finger
caught in a car-door
and I missed school for it,
once a fire ant bit
my toe and I missed
school for it

hold something for me,
a needle pointing upwards,
a bear-shaped bottle of honey,
a crushed cd, a cup of salt-water

pull my body out of the bottle
    I've come to tell a joke:

en esta luz parezco ser espuma,
ser construido de bromas, así vengo, es verdad, pero
en la noche, cuando cambia la luz, me
convierto en un edificio, espuma -> edificio,
espuma -> edificio

protein;
polyester opening;
sand shredding;
hollow, white beetles burrowing out
hollow, glass flies
a protein;
ants in a plaster ceiling
water fills it
zigzagging pills
full of water
one moment not another
water fills it
one orange
light beaming out
of a long, blue carpet
if I
find a mattress
in the middle
of the gulf
does that make
me Columbus?

If I could prove you wrong
phoenix of sand
"vertical living"
I aspire to joystick control
of a crab walking
forwards

drowning on
the turnpike
leaping off
the turnpike

Is this the miracle of the inventing mind? Really? Island nations and coastal cities close to drowning in the ocean? As a species we can invent anything and have, do anything and have, but the whole time, the thousands of years we've done it, this is its byproduct? I am trying not to show it but I am enraged. I feel cheated by consequences I cannot fully comprehend. I feel guilty enough in causation but unequipped to remedy my/our actions. This is a deep and slow rage, one that I can't fully feel at any precise moment, but one that flatly spreads across the present and possibility.

I saw Caroline Bergvall in a lecture at the University of Pennsylvania say that the sea, back when it was the primary area for migration, used to have a connotation attached to it of being a space of language change, where one culture became another. She said that there was a time period in the later 20th century where this connotation seemed to go away, especially with the popularity of flight and driving. She mentions, however, that recent events in the world have caused this connotation to return, albeit in a stranger form, with high-profile news stories about Somali pirates, migrants stranded in bodies of water due to conflicting and racist laws, Caribbean immigration (like the Elián González story). The sea for her is a place where language is destroyed and made, it is full of languages and letters in flux or in danger. That is the premise of *Drift*.

In a film called *Kwassa Kwassa* by SUPERFLEX, a narrating voice (Soumette Ahmed) from the Comoro Islands says "Perhaps you can't eat identity…Identity will always eat you. Like the ocean. The ocean eats everything."

I want to wonder the following publicly. The ocean is a manifestation of the unknown and the changing, the imperceptibly far and deep, and it is also monstrous in both reality and text. Miami gains its unique cultural/language construction from a traversal of the surface of the ocean. What happens, then, when that which produces Miami, the ocean, covers it? Swallows it? Fills it?

there isn't even an
inch of rainwater in my
purse yet but little
plants are growing
the starting stem of a strangler fig
in my wallet
and the red-yellow leaf of a croton
by the tic-tacs

RADIO Y LAGUITO

Radio y Laguito

para Sara June Woods

Aquí todo está compuesto
por radios
o laguitos
radio o laguito

por todo Miami hay
radios o laguitos
exactamente cuál y cuántos hay
depende de
la hora

y de cuanta
vida ha sido temor y
cuanto humor y del
color del árbol más cercano
y también depende
de los hábitos de niños y hombres
del color de sus calzoncillos y de
los amigos y de la violencia y
del barrio

los radios expendan y escuchan
transfieren y subliman
murmuran así
"habhabhabhabhab"
y cantan así
"habhabhabhabhab"
como helicóptero

tienen metal duro
y parecen estar hechos con
papel cuadriculado
mi abuelo es un radio
mi padre fue un radio
mi hermano es un radio
este libro lo escribiría
un radio el techo es muchos
radios escondidos

encuentro
laguitos por las calles
en mis manos laguitos
llueve laguitos
como un bistec de laguitos
empiezo a lavar laguitos
como si fueran ropa
abro la ventana y veo
un laguito y me doy cuenta
que puedo convertirme en un bote
y cruzar el laguito para alcanzar
a otro laguito y
lo encuentro
y me encanta
y al fondo del laguito hay un radio
tocando Bola de Nieve

me siento como Patroclo
mirando a un radio
nautilo de metal
me da dolor de
cabeza siento
que el cuerpo
me empieza a rezumar
algodón me siento

liberado de algo
los radios transmiten
los sonidos del exiliado
suena como raspar
cartas de juego con
las uñas

y los laguitos
brillan y enferman
y cambian de color

una mujer habla
con su vecino
un hombre con
bastón con
dolores de artritis y
la mujer tiene el pelo
pintado ambos
son radios
ambos participan

hablan de sus hijos
laguitos
y como siguen
en sus clases y
cuan grandes son y
mientras tanto
los hijos juegan con
laguitos
usan sus dedos para
hacer ondulaciones
sus nombres
agua en agua
cuando están solos
allí entre las piernas

encuentran otro laguito
mastican otro laguito
caminan de gota
en gota

con el radio
se construye la casa
y con el radio se inunda
seis pulgadas de agua

al fondo del mar
hay un laguito

arriba del edificio
hay un laguito

en la superficie del agua
hay miles de radios
que cambian de idioma
con las olas

en el lobby de un
hotel hay un radio
que toca una canción

la canción es laguito

no es un secreto
que los idiomas
son triángulos

en la costa nos transformamos

qué decimos si
la costa se empieza a mover

si la costa entra a la casa
o entra al trabajo
si en un momento
nuestra familia está sentada
en un banco de arena
y sólo podemos comunicarnos
por radio

grito para que
el agua de un laguito
pueda traer mi voz
a otro mundo

en clase la matemática
es laguito

abro la ventana
la abro otra vez
continúo abriéndola
hasta que lo creo
hasta que pasa el año
un año de mucho dolor

el primero de enero
es un laguito

Lunar

esponja / la mía /
comestible / particular /
si habremos / y hoy / lo posible /
esponja / y un lunar sobre
el hombro / sobra / imagen del
blanqueo del coral / sombra /
esponja / cambia / el armario es
el mío y es de madera / enjuago el lunar
lo enjuago

Patroclo

algunos escudos /
parecimos hechos de arcilla /
mi ex-novio y yo / y con
cada día / un laguito se expande
entre nosotros

Esponja

el internet me hace sentir horrible, como si
todo pasara a la misma vez, y como si hubiera 30
horas en el día / casco del demonio / ciruela /
avenidas y malas noticias / dominó / dibujo el
mundo sobre un papel / duermo adentro del congelador /
encuentro parte de un radio en el patio / lo siembro /
allí crece un manicomio / azul y marrón /
en seis semanas / azul y marrón /
ciruela / una uva entre los labios de Patroclo /
en seis semanas todas estas ideas
serán ahogadas / serán fluidas /
al dibujo le añado agua de una esponja

Enfoque

una burbuja entra a la casa
con un niño pegando gritos / los padres
se enfocan / el niño pasa la burbuja
entre platos hondos llenos de agua /
va del uno al otro al otro / los padres se enfocan /
esta es tu ciencia / mundos particulares /
globos / deposita la burbuja donde
crecen hongos / y el niño desaparece /
los padres se enfocan

Miami

en la frente me dibujo
un laguito / como un tercer ojo /
porque siempre he sido un milagro /
mate psíquico / esta familia
viene de fábrica / di de baja /
no estoy seguro / alivios de
mis dolores / mi padre es un radio
escondido en el aire / hablamos
bastante sobre Cuba

LOSING MIAMI

III.

I designed this mystery to be heavy
grieving against earwigs
my lived-in routines
I'm desperate for a blow up in my life

I catered to threadbearers
because of lack of confidence
let my fingers be oily
in this surface dream

I put my shoulder to my mother's
hoping for a frog to distract
us in our TV commercial
we're a carnival at home

water is rising
that's the obvious
but the hardest is to concede treasures
to an imaginary coastline

I'd be the boyfriend of future-telling
that's the obvious
but I set my sponge aside
mark full as full

garden of walls
saluted, salted
78-degree winter, thought of it
city eats rumors
the winter of them
I write evil things
about the water
become Luxembourg, unopposed
psychic tissue paper floating on
the water as it nears my favorite restaurant
cut it with huge scissors, like an opening
ribbon, taping the ocean shut
I baked a batch yesterday
for friends who didn't like them
government makes a garden of walls
and flings it into the weather

middle of the life I lied into

smooth stone in a bottle

the movie playing in our heads

countries I haven't been to

imagine them all glass pinecones

carried a dictator shoulder-saddled across streams

marry a boatman

a movie playing in my head

9 days long, and romantic

miel y agua, aceite y vela
cardamomo y manzanilla
frijoles y alcohol, lavanda y rosa
anís y caracol, anís y caracol
anís y caracol, anís y caracol

ruego por nosotros
ahora y en un "ahora" escondido

sincrética allowance pájaro steak dar
criminal coraje water tendida field debajo
salted mar virus sigue giant carabela city
palma awful infección girls abierta bluer
grama palms sudan rafter mariquita heat
boca agape el great mosquito summons
coraje and viento acid pueblo gridlines
pobreza dreaming Haití they mandan
back queman back pobreza back abierta
back rezo that no take mi sweet vida back

maestro sea usted crippled arbol beast de coal burbuja upside contrato sea lata of sardinas the argumento comptroller la border el sea niño scales pared falls desde precipice fondo sea crece below se becomes monstro brings oceano with vida destroys ciudad touches sed become madre against monstro clear agua tells futuro then mi occupation está committedly muriendo god rezo don't llévame to demonio

apocalypse tuyo is mental and dental never
jamás contribute resisto gravity ningunas
witches en this jardín bring oceano back
crueldad milk momento dream toro kills
amigo the oceano kills amigo tomorrow
toro kills mar kills mañana throw plástico
into boca of cielo throw plástico into boca
of mañana bull mata set virus into coral
imagine caballitos rising superficie pray que
bury mis eager desperdicios in sonido

lovers at the bottom of the ocean
necklace at the bottom of the ocean
shipwrecks at the bottom of the ocean
corpses at the bottom of the ocean
all myths, ningún fondo de las cosas
malagredecidas, no bottom to a hell-bat
not a sink nor a belly crease

stolen static in the middle of the
dripping cotton in the middle of the
life at rest in the middle of the
birth of iron in the middle of the
undressing in the middle of the

'YO' QUIERE DECIR SUNBURN

‘Yo’ Quiere Decir Sunburn

la lámpara
magnífica quiere decir
altura y pasteurized
yo quiere decir sunburn yo
también lavo el único núcleo
tuyo as if matte hair was
pasture y sí, sí me llevan pal
rinconcito de esa luna hay
lunatic morons una fila my
toenails sizzling over popping
cedar esta vez no, como si
yo quisiera hablar de mal humor
mata la planta prenup a
clogged city that flower
is whiter than mine it’s
a feathery comforter
no hubiera frito las manos si
no viviera en la casa doblada
yo quiero traerte pero yo quiere
decir sunburn y allí es donde
me tranco; tal, tal, tal
esa luna, esa, esa

Avispaaaaaa

el tornillo, la herramienta
que imagina lo que es ser
casado, thrown like
a shotput, just a
dance away hay una
avispaaaaaaaaaaaaaa
no confío en el cuarto no
aterrizo en Maryland di a
luz la luz, esta, esta luz
I am embarrassed as I am every
Tuesday to speak twice
no mi placer pero
mi boca, transformada
de otra manera en Marilyn
it smells like crusty nothing el Uber
que me encuentra en
la calle 16 y Lombard, esta
vez yo soy el edificio

Parade: Motorcade

I chewed strings, thought
how did my life become a banana
and returned to the game
y claro que siento mucho
orgullo por Mónica
pero la lavanda no es hijo
de puta, ni dientes,
punch-drunk,
el techo es un
casco borracho, bordado en
ciencia, vino y aceite
he came and sated my
cat's hunger
but not mine, burn
victims are burned
I am a sheep
esto es la lógica
pura de
un desfile

Mujeriego

los hombres de mi
familia son murciélagos
y yo una muñeca tiesa
con nalgas naranjas
el crotón es de
Madagascar the parade
unstable as dimes
ya, ya encima de la
guagua tomo a Tomás
como camello
this eyebrow is select, unlike
divots, a womanizer
is a box of jars
que lástima
ser manatí y a veces
cruzar la calle

Sunburn

patina i griega
el calor patina
my tissue shoulders
this pink, that one
my birth was
not a boat I parried
it was just
skating, si ser anónimo
y nacional me
viene fácilmente es
porque me faltan las
facultades the donkey
I assume is a friend is not
that is a sunburn
la i griega nos
viene como algodón
that ribbon in
my window is how
I speak back to the
yard, I pull, and the
yard pulls back

Pato

yo soy inseguro and secular
like moths, I would corroborate
any story given about
my childhood, my bellybutton
sé de todos los
chismes, soy un pato
con dos narices
una en cada lenguaje
I run away from
my rivers, imagine
holes in sandwiches
my cousin is not true
ni es tan
hermoso como dicen
los cubiertos, pero
este aguacate es
un perro y mi madre
es un milagro don't
ask me for a post-it
note, I use them
as reminders

Iron Grass

la espina me conviene
la sal, la sala certainly
a point in space is divided
as are my gloves, vengo
de un estado condenado
a convertirse en algas, the
iron grass, the wish of
a booming coast
I am at the edge
of my skin thinking
these pores could
fit a boat in them
este hierro se inunda
esta hierba se inunda
esta manera de ser
it is called titration

Quemada

I have laid moss over
a cup, called a friend
drunk and yelled at
something, been somewhere
I did not recall, known
someone and forgotten them

un tipo me trae
la tráquea en
una bandeja (ojalá que
el agua no sea tan lúcida),
tiene una
sonrisa pasteurizada,
me dice "¡buenas!"
y me sirve el
órgano
it is
summer
and my dreams are
full of flies

I would
pardon
him, though
I would

Nieve de Miami

my lung is a critical
thing, tender like veal
it is a record player

that moon, there
trae nieve
mucha nieve

y se derrite
y nadamos otra vez

my lung is sweet like veal
my eyes are round like a record player

esa luna, esa
se derrite
y nadamos
nadamos
y cambiamos de
lenguaje como
monjes

is that right
to remeet a
high school friend
as if he was
certainly volatile

y él trae nieve
y se derrite

Ricky Ricardo is my Bedazzled Mom

I'm an idiot implant
un disparate
in a three room home

***

just as I thought a bunch
of cement-snatchers
barging into my
fireplace

you've told
me lots of crazy
stories in your
life but this is
the craziest

a violet smoking robe the
pucker of applause
they clap for your ass
stuck in a heavy
material bucket hairy
Cubans in love

your frowzy pendulum
in John Wayne's heart
as whited-out as a condo
and fast double-sided
like beating

is my footprint
amazing

keep my career
boatmen

is that my pocketbook
on your head what
penmanship laugh
into orange head
we the island come out of
trouble every time

por QUÉ por QUÉ esta mujer
siempre forma algo and you say
he probably didn't say
woopdy-doo don't go around
calling me no more

my slap-stick double tongue
it's the devil of leaving you
the oaf I'm the yelling oaf
the straight-haired one
that's plenty 'scuse for me

can you fill the
tub with chocolate so
we can be on with our lives
in another place
another year
it is Febreeary before
winter ends

que cómico te parece
yo ir de un árbol
al otro como un mono

the baby is coming into
how tough the money is

what if I wear the apron
this month people I place
stay put in my
corner-store I'd be a lamb
for you

Batista is the mustache
agency's pbx operator
I want to
dance with you
in the same
design
I'm a dipper
from way back

in levity
it's like a volcano
and a broom
blue ridicule

it is not a
myth that I have
upset Lucy
it is categorical

ginormous couch is pregnant
forget about me

my father
eats roast beef
I'm a rainbow
roll but
am definitely not
a baby at the coast

muchacho y también
estoy en tu banda

me and my boys
are dominos in suits
Lucy's my interior
reporter

in Havana
the reason for action
is like marrow

slinking across
the conveyer belt
is a bedazzled turd
high-speed
my wife wraps it
in white blankets
and donates it to the church

is this really all
my three cameras
can put together
I have come so far to
be left here in the living room
or with little pollitos
Fred's love-affair
with waistlines
my out-of-stock
dormitory

I have one
bed and you
have another
that is how the
ocean should be too

I’m not even the cousin
of a boat-lifter but I met
one when I was dizzy
on a Saturday night

they call me Cuban Pete
I’m the king of the rumba beat
when I play the maracas
everything goes
chick-chiky boom
chick-chiky boom

BETTER ORGANIZED

Category 1

Every day an attachment, rain
the hands in drains, my toes
purulent, turbulent, I torrent
movies slowly, as I greet a category 1
loving containers, mistaking apples
it's applesauce I've dreamed of
the excuse for a roof
every day that hum, the category 1
easy wind's leopard bumps, the small
inconveniences, what's a bit of
rain to a city overcome
underdressed, ineluctable
where the good news is
a day exists inside of
turbulent good news
I'm used to at least eight category 1s
a year, June to November
but this, this is a category 1
this is rain, I'm marbles
I'm thumbtacks, that eager
eye, a breath without numb
I hum, a category 1 is not
enough to lift the ocean
and pour it into my pants
at least not here, but it
can evaluate a coast, and set it
aside, or it can destroy New
York, but even I can destroy
New York

Goad

in the middle of the
road I'm goaded on by
an SUV, my teeth
its color, but I ignore it
the early wind, the animal
alarm, inside my
home the lizards come in
bend sidewalks, a body, a map
the car drives through
my door, white door
more lizards, more wind
gets in, I split my list
drown the kids, eat a steak
the early wind for a
category 4, it's been a
long time coming, this storm
this woman in a car, the baseball
no matter, watch the clock
as if one wire could
wrap the table, marble
fixtures, weighty
punches, me and the engine
this is it, I've been waiting
the car is in love, the king is thin
the early air, animal alarm,
do massive trees grow
to goad me on?

Sandbag

I wish a hurricane were
more dramatic, came with
sandbags seething in
spin, hit citizens with sandbags
to displace them, a category
runs away, bruised-stomached citizens
with a surplus of sandbags and now
the block is its own levy full of
open or sealed sandbags, the
Godzilla we always wanted, thought would
come sooner, well I slept through
a category 3, felt it was okay, but
woke up and the yard was full of sandbags
my shutters were dented, that's how
open I am to change, it's a sign
of my dateability, I knew Wilma way
before she arrived, the left
compliments, cracked ginger ale
and a sandbag the size of my cousin
rolling across US-1, nowhere exactly
to be, but has to be there at 7
with meat already on
the grill, Wilma is
a water pitcher—lemonade—
no, I meant, lemonade

Better Organized

snow is sport
divided snow
I place a
ward to light
against grass,
set the pitch,
remember it
doesn't snow, that
that was something
seen in the
mirror under the cup
I've seen snow
revolved snow
a napkin on
the hood of a car
"just" frost—
lit frost
real adults
have
activities
I have snow
and put snow
in a thermos
dye my hair
feed my pets
turn off the A/C
and chew on snow
hard-earned pissed-on snow

and though the
outlets are purple
Matthew has just
organized into
a category 4

Angel

the natural environment here is a pageant
of self-destruction but a mangrove is an
instrument of regrowth and recombination
insinuating, not insinuating what I think
you're insinuating: the Frankenstein growth
of a hurricane moving over Granada eating
houses and animals from the islands, resting
them on the Keys' little heads I will go crazy enough
as a magazine, if it's a magazine you're after
but along I-95 a hurricane is lying to me
it's hot like forever and always and there
is a hurricane coming along and that's just
enough to get me out of bed, a star shivers
a clover pivots, a lizard enters, and that's that
the pageant, insinuating that the city has vomited
and I'm a magazine finally with a story
to tell all the young boys about
knuckle-cracking
as if it were my job
and I was
a palm tree's angel

Parmalat

Monday is made for a garbage man, as wind comes
red and green behind you, good luck
a basement is made up of 40 barrels of water
and 20 cartons of Parmalat for family, in avenues
across the living room, true north, so called
here finds milk forever to tell you the truth
while I find absolute pleasure in
not being outside, Monopoly, saltines
just past the gorgeous window
metaled-over
is a bottle of crystalline debt

Out of the Air

he shoots chunks of gold out
of the air, orbiters, to say
"wet heartland" on a pink station
I'm going crazy with the news, gusts
imagining my husband is the eye, where rooms
are quiet and yawning, hacky sack-eyed monsters
riding rain into my attic, my basement is
a puzzle box of limestone and water, so
casually a cactus as to be disregarded, they're sending
through my window a postcard
with little red
handwriting that says "July 26th is a myth"

Glass

as you asked before, I grew up made
of silkscreen with a glass brother, swept
our hair to the left and absorbed ash, said this is
the wind, left the room, we sailed again
he is floorless, zinc, vulnerable to morals
toothy, and covered in canyons, we both
have to laugh at the idea of our
father in a windstorm, I have a headache
it's not even close to nighttime, phony
maneuvers, dirty clothes
sulfur for the cheeks
50$ and a license plate for this embalming
of the Coriolis effect

Visitors

Mistake took me for a liar, drew string
from my neck, waterform, rubber man
flailing across the window, opened up
my lower back to the bite of fire ants
a circle is wide, a storm
in a shoebox, fever set into my shoulders
I play a board game with my mom, in the half-dark
of the afternoon, exchanging paper bills
animal alarm, with this one goes the roof
like a bottle cap, the letters "th" and "sh" surrounding
the sound of a train inside the sound of a larger train
marbled, gold-plated trains,
during the board game she says "when a train
passes by, run quick into the visitors' bathroom"

Elation of the Outside

the shell of a crystal ego
laughed out lunch meat
christ's open eyelid, a ficus
my way over into a tropical
storm full as a fish
it brought Granada with it, opened
book pages, lingerie, the motor
of a cartoon closet to keep my heart in
I'm getting closer, a category 4
this isn't like Andrew, it's duller
moth candle—green and obsolete
only miracle of carbon so far
two handshakes to say that
when I'm in my house, in the wind
shutters closed, lights off
I'm not me, I'm my absolute value

LOSING MIAMI

IV.

we borrowed vodka from off-stage squares
spent time pushing each other
drew straws to puke
    left notes on each other's forearms
                happened to matter
                judged each other
                got angry
drew weed on backs while I watched
                        thanked jesus
drank and drank
          insulted strangers
          put it in plastic bottles
                waited violet dreams off-stage
                slept in 3 sheets
                scaled parking lots
I have a puzzle and a handful of tops
white rum and a handful of tops

as people in my life die I have
bad dreams

my head gets as small as my stomach

I see sheep in all the days I
don't realize

a golden hand, wrapping paper

between islands, pronounces potion
    let it be a weed in the drawers, stopped
    hammering particles into clothing
    had the water isolate itself in his throat
        that's the river
        I said
        no that's the river
        that one
        absolutely
        I thought it was…
        no it's that
                I put a capsule
            back in his throat
        suck the water back up
    pop the bubble that is choking him
  it grew blue in my room
it absolutely wished to be bigger

puts a nest on a higher branch

1) Imagine the loss of something small.

2) Imagine the loss of something about your size.

3) Imagine the loss of something very large.

At different points in my life, I have considered these questions differently, told myself that small things were as huge as I made them in my spirit, and that the large could be made small. A watch and a house were similarly sized if I instructed them to be. This is still true, but I have never asked myself "will not having a watch make me strange" or "where will I put myself if I don't have a watch" or "what will my mother do if I lose my watch" or "what watch will I be wearing tonight when everyone in the world is wearing theirs?"

an heirloom day, started slowly
gets a track of anger through its center
in reaction to one's own appetite
steadily impossible and sinking

I give this and other
particles to my son
who is laying on the beach

Appendix

porque el lenguaje también naufraga
este secreto te lo doy
pero no entero
ni con buena fe

LOSING MIAMI / PERDER MIAMI

pg 18

only plastic
survives
like always

so forms a meringue
out of bottles on the water

pg 19

I cheat on the door
I rip holes in the door with my horns

the ocean abbreviates
traces

pg 20

the plane
the plane
waaaaaaaaaaaaaaasp

pg 52

in this light it looks like I'm foam,
I'm made of jokes, that's how I come, it's true, but
at night, when the light changes,
I turn into a building, foam -> building,
foam -> building

pg 74

honey and water, oil and candle
cardamom and chamomile
beans and alcohol, lavender and rose
anise and seashell, anise and seashell
anise and seashell, anise and seashell

I pray for us
now and in a hidden "now"

pg 75-77

syncretic concesión bird bistec give / criminal courage agua stretched prado / below salado sea virus follows gigante / caravel ciudad palm atroz infection / niñas open azul grass palmas sweat / balcero faggot calor mouth abierto the / gran mosquito convoca courage y / wind ácido town cuadrícula poverty / soñando Haiti ellos send de vuelta / burn de vuelta poverty de vuelta open / de vuelta pray que don't devuelvas my dulce life

teacher mar you lisiado tree bestia / of carbón bubble revés contract mar can / de sardines el argument contralor / the frontera the mar boy escala wall cae / from precipicio deep mar grows bajo / it hace monster trae ocean / con life destrue city toca thirst / hacerse mother contra monster claro / water cuenta future entonces my ocupación / it's comprometidamente dying dios pray / no me take al devil

apocalipsis yours es mental y dental / nunca never contribuir resist gravedad / no brujas in este garden trae / ocean de vuelta cruelty leche moment / sueño bull mata friend el ocean mata / friend mañana bull mata sea mata / tomorrow tirar plastic en mouth de / sky tirar plastic en mouth de / tomorrow toro kills colocar virus en coral / imaginar seahorses subiendo surface ruego / that entierres my ansioso rubbish en sound

crío esta luna es tuya
y de tu hijo
nunca lo transfieres

child this moon is yours
it's for splitting in half
again and again

RADIO Y LAGUITO / RADIO AND LITTLE LAKE

Radio and Little Lake

Here everything is composed
of radios
or little lakes
radio or little lake

throughout Miami there are
radios or little lakes
exactly which and how many there are
depends on
the time of day

and how much
of life has been terror and

how much humor and on
the color of the closest tree
and it depends also
on the habits of children and men
the color of their underwear and on
friends and on violence and
on the neighborhood

radios expend and listen
they transfer and sublimate
they murmur like this
"habhabhabhabhab"
and they sing like this
"habhabhabhabhab"
like a helicopter
they have hard metal
and they seem to be made of
graph paper
my grandfather is a radio
my father was a radio
my brother is a radio
this book would be written
by a radio the roof is many
hidden radios

I find
little lakes through the streets
in my hand little lakes
it rains little lakes
I eat a little lake steak
I start washing little lakes
as if they were clothes
I open the window and I see
a little lake and I notice
I can make myself into a boat
and cross the little lake to reach
another little lake and
I find it
and I love it

and at the bottom of the little lake is a radio
playing Bola de Nieve

I feel like Patroclus
looking at a radio
metal nautilus
it gives me
a headache I feel
my body ooze
cotton I feel
relieved of something
the radios transmit
the sounds of the exile
it sounds like scratching
playing cards with
your nails

and the little lakes
glow and make you sick
and they change color

a woman talks
with her neighbor
a man with
a cane with
arthritis pains and
the woman has dyed
hair both
are radios
both participate

they talk about their kids
little lakes
and how are
their classes and
how big are they and
meanwhile
the kids are playing with
little lakes

they use their fingers to
make waves
their names
water in water
when they are alone
there between their legs
is another little lake
they chew another little lake
they walk from drop
to drop

with the radio
a house is built
and with the radio it floods
6 inches of water

at the bottom of the sea
there is a little lake

at the top of the building
there is a little lake

on the surface of the water
there are thousands of radios
that change language
with the waves

in the lobby of a
hotel there is a radio
playing a song

the song is a little lake

it is not a secret
that languages
are triangles

on the coast we transform

what do we say if

the coast starts moving
if the coast enters our home
or our workplace
if in one moment
our family is seated
on a sandbar
and we can only speak
by radio

I scream so that
the water of a little lake
can take my voice
to another world

at school mathematics
is a little lake

I open the window
I open it again
I keep opening it
until I believe it
until the year passes
a year of much pain

the first of January
is a little lake

Mole

sponge / mine /
edible / particular /
if we had / and today / the possible /
sponge / and a mole on
the shoulder / is left over / an image
of coral bleaching / shadow /
sponge / changes / the dresser is
mine and its made of wood / I rinse the mole
I rinse it

Patroclus

some shields /
we seem to be made of wax /
my ex-boyfriend and I / and with
every day / a lake expands
between us

Sponge

the internet makes me feel horrible, as if
everything happened at the same time, and as if there were 30
hours in a day / demon's helmet / cherry /
avenues and bad news / dominoes / I draw the
world on paper / I sleep in the freezer /
I find part of a radio in the yard / I plant it /
there grows an asylum / blue and brown /
in six weeks / blue and brown /
cherry / a grape in between the lips of Patroclus /
in six weeks all these ideas
will be drowned / will be fluid /
I add sponge water to the drawing

Focus

a bubble enters the house
with a boy screaming his head off / the parents
focus / the boy passes the bubble
between bowls full of water /
it goes from one to another to another / the parents focus /
this is your science / particular worlds
balloons / he deposits the bubble where
fungus grows / and the boy disappears /
the parents focus

Miami

on my forehead I draw
a little lake / like a third eye /
because I've always been a miracle
psychic yerba mate / this family
comes from the factory / I dismissed /
I'm not sure / reliefs of
my pains / my father is a radio
hidden in the air / we speak
quite a bit of Cuba

como una piedra
o una orquestra
cada mierda se une

cada minuto se inunda

'Yo' Quiere Decir Sunburn / 'I' Means Quemada

'I' Means Quemada

the amazing
lamp means
height and pasteurizado
I means quemada I
also wash your only nucleus
como si pelo mate fuera
prado and yes, yes they take me
to the corner of that moon there are
idiotas lunáticos a line mis
uñas chisporroteandos sobre
el cedro this time no, as if

I wanted to discuss bad attitude
kill the plant prenupcial para una
ciudad atrancada esa flor
es más blanca que la mía es
un edredón de plumas
I wouldn't have fried my hands if
I didn't live in the doubled house   *the dubbed house*   *the folded house*
I want to bring you but I means
quemada and that's where
I get stuck; such, such, such
that moon, that one, that one

Waaaaaasp

the nail, the tool
that imagines what it is to
be married, lanzado como
un peso, solo un baile
de distancia there is
a waaaaaaaaaaaaaasp
I don't confide in the room don't
land in Maryland I gave to light   *I gave birth to light*
the light, this, this light
estoy avergonzado como lo estoy cada
Martes de hablar dos veces
not my pleasure but
my mouth, transformed
by other means into Marilyn
huele como una nada costrosa the Uber
that meets me on
16th and Lombard, this
time I am the building

Desfile

mastiqué cuerdas, pensé
cómo se convirtió mi vida en guineo

y volví al juego
and obviously I feel a lot of
pride for Mónica
but lavender is not a son
of a bitch, nor are teeth,
embobado,
the roof is a
drunken helmet, sewn into *drunken shell* *drunken shard*
science, wine and oil
vino y sació el
hambre de mi gata
pero no el mio, víctimas
de quemaduras están quemadas
yo soy oveja
this is the pure
logic of
a parade

Womanizer

the men in my
family are bats
and I'm a stiff wrist
with orange buttcheeks
the croton is from
Madagascar el desfile
inestable como monedas
now, now on top of
the bus I drink Tomás *take Tomás*
like a camel
esta ceja es selecta, no como
terrones, un mujeriego
es una caja de jarras
what a shame
to be a manatee and sometimes
cross the street

Quemada

skate Y *patina greek I*
the heat skates
mi tejido carga *mis hombros de pañuelo*
esta rosada, esa
mi nacimiento no
fue bote yo rechazé *pare*
solo fue
patina, if being anonymous
and national comes
easily to me its
because I lack the
faculties el burro
que asumo es mi amigo no lo es
eso es una quemada
the Y comes *the greek I*
to us like cotton
esa cinta en
mi ventana es como
contesto el
patio, yo jalo, y el
patio jala de vuelta

Duck *Fag*

I'm insecure y seglar
como las polillas, yo corroboraría
cualquier cuento sobre mi
infancia, mi ombligo
I know about every
joke, I'm a fag
with two noses
one in each language
huyo de mis
rios, imagina
huecos en bocadillos

mi primo no es verdad
nor is he so
beautiful like the
utensils say he is, but
this avocado is
a dog and my mother
is a miracle no me
pidas post-its
los uso como
recordatorios

Hierba de Hierro

the spine is convenient to me
salt, living room claro que
un punto en espacio se divide
como mis guantes, I come
from a state condemned to
be converted into algae, la
hierba de hierro, el deseo de
una costa en auge
estoy al borde
de mi piel pensando
estos poros podrían
caber un bote en ellos
this iron drowns
this grass drowns
this way of being
se llama valoración

Sunburn

He puesto musgo sobre
el vaso, he llamado un amigo
borracho y he gritado
a algo, he estado en algun lugar

que no recuerdo, he conocido a
alguien y lo he olvidado

some guy brings me
my trachea on
a platter (god-willing
water is not so lucid)
he has a
pasteurized smile,
he says to me "hello!"
and serves me the
organ
es
verano
y mis sueños están
llenos de moscas

pero le
perdonaría
sí, yo
lo haría

Miami Snow

mi pulmón es algo
crítico, tierno como la ternera
es un tocadiscos

esa luna, esa
it brings snow
so much snow

and it melts
and we swim again

mi pulmón es dulce como ternera
mis ojos son redondos como un tocadiscos

that moon, there

it melts
and we swim
we swim
and change
languages like
monks

eso está bien
reconocer un
amigo de escuela secundaria
como si fuera
ciertamente volátil

and he brings snow
and he melts *and it melts*

Ricky Ricardo Habla de Si Mismo
En Un Inglés Perfecto y Condenado

Lucy, this transplant is being rejected
Lucy, do you also see the two other Ricky's
on my right and left
one taller one shorter
I'm beginning to think one of them is your husband

Acknowledgements

I first have to thank those I grew up with and continue to speak with and share this life with. You know who you are. This book is for you.

Thank you to the poets who gave me advice/reading recommendations for this book at different stages of its creation, including but not limited to Mario Alejandro Ariza, Raquel Salas Rivera, CA Conrad, Angel Dominguez, Mark Johnson, and Orchid Tierney. Raquel deserves more note, as their reading of an earlier version of this manuscript, and their publication of some of the very first poems from this book in *The Wanderer*, helped me sharpen my thinking and little by little grow this book. Their understanding of the Caribbean has been absolutely essential to this writing.

Thank you to Janice Lee for believing in this book and allowing me creative freedom with how the manuscript could approach a non-Spanish-speaking reader. Few editors would trust the language fragmentation that drives this book. Thank you as well to the full team of the Accomplices, especially Chiwan Choi.

Thank you to the editors of *Hinchas de Poesia*, *the tiny*, *Acentos Review*, *Sinking City*, *Tender Loin*, *Deluge*, *The Wanderer*, and *Esferas*, where pieces from this book first appeared.

Thank you to the Philadelphia poetry community. This is the first book I will be publishing not as a Philadelphia resident;

this is something that weighs heavy on my heart.

Thank you to my mother who did not want to move her family to Miami, but who built us a home there. Thank you to my grandparents who did not want to move to the United States, but who built us a home there.

Thank you to Jibreel for making a home with me.

This book is a thank you to Cuban exiles and their kids.

Gabriel Ojeda-Sagué is a gay, Latino Leo raised in Miami, currently living in Chicago. He is the author of the poetry books *Jazzercise is a Language* (The Operating System, 2018), on the exercise craze of the 1980s, and *Oil and Candle* (Timeless, Infinite Light, 2016), on ritual and racism. He is also the author of chapbooks on gay sex, Cher, the Legend of Zelda, and anxious bilingualism. His third book, *Losing Miami*, on the potential sinking of Miami due to climate change and sea level rise, is published in 2019 by CCM/The Accomplices. He is currently a PhD candidate in English at the University of Chicago.

OFFICIAL

THE ACCOMPLICES

GET OUT OF JAIL

* VOUCHER *

- -

Tear this out.

Skip that social event.

It's okay.

You don't have to go if you don't want to. Pick up the book you just bought. Open to the first page. You'll thank us by the third paragraph.

If friends ask why you were a no-show, show them this voucher.

You'll be fine.

- -

We're thriving.